SCALLYWAG

Confessions of a multi-mom

Jacoba Combrinck

Published by FastPencil

Published by FastPencil
3131 Bascom Ave.
Suite 150
Campbell CA 95008 USA
info@fastpencil.com
(408) 540-7571
(408) 540-7572 (Fax)
http://www.fastpencil.com

Second Edition

For Marietjie, David and all the children and staff at Owl.

꿩

Acknowledgments

I thank my family for their unwavering support and patience.
The team at FastPencil made the publication process smooth.

Contents

Introduction

I am a multi-mom, which means to me that I play in multiple teams. First, the wonderful RIM team, as a programmer/analyst, which I love; second the Combrinck team, where I am Mom, Doctor, Chef, Partner, Friend; finally the K-W (Kitchener-Waterloo) team, where I belong to a most warm and welcoming community.

Naturally my thoughts are filled with stories from my action-filled plays in all the paths I happily tread.

Since many of my musings come from moments with my son, I wanted to include a few of my favourite poems about childhood, by Rabindranath Tagore. His work finds a connection with my own, although I would not be so bold as to place myself in his league as a poet. I also took the liberty of adding my own illustrations of his touching verses.

Haven

Century

You run on your small strong legs,
confidently scramble up carpeted stairs, giggling
as your father tries to grab you
As I rub cream on you, I know these soft limbs of yours
will become a man's legs
They will carry you to 2100, where I will never go

Journey

As you sleep in your car seat, your small busy hands are still
Chubby fingers and dimples in rosy soft skin are still
Clear and pitched voice is still
Long eyelashes move slightly, tender mouth, smiling, is still
Are you dreaming of some joy in play?

Birthday

Peaceful home-day, family-day, heart-day
Joy-day, play-day, small-boy-hug-day
Chocolate-cake-day, candles-blow-day
Peaceful home-day, family-day, love-day

Baby to Boy

You pull me out of myself,
tug at the ends of my strength.
Nurturing you brings challenges never imagined;
Loving you brings joy never known

September Day

Before the early morning light
You call to me for a hug
Small arms reach as I kiss soft cheeks
Fluffy duvet still warm from the night

My blonde boy with your silky hair
You giggle when I tickle your back
Your dad comes in and you beam
Snuggle for a moment in the rocking chair

Reach

Snowflake

Last night we read in your nature book about snowflakes
You looked at the picture with wide eyes,
amazed that they are one of a kind

This morning we cuddle for a few moments in the lightening dawn
I whisper that you are my snowflake, no one else is just like you
You smile: "Thank you Mamma,
and you are my beaudiful budderfly"

Castle

Blue triangles, red squares
Stack the blocks to make stairs
Towers and turrets, up they go
Just one more - oh!

Heap of triangles, red squares
Try again, make higher stairs
Towers and turrets, just so
There we are - wo!

Sick Day

You wake at four and call to me
Small face flushed and small body hot
Milk and medicine soothes until seven

Cheeks still warm, eyes bright
you quietly watch treasured stories
while Mamma works nearby

Hands

Small fingers, smooth palms
Resting on the pillow next to me

Small gentle breath, soft sighs
On the pillow next to me

Small sleepy hand, reaches and grasps
Caresses my hair on the pillow with me

Bubbles

Creamy porridge, nutritious treat
eaten with a promise of bubbles -
young, picky eater enjoys his cereal,
then runs outside to make pearly,
soapy, floaty orbs that drift in the air
settle on the grass just long enough for tiny feet to pop,
small voice squealing in delight

Embrace

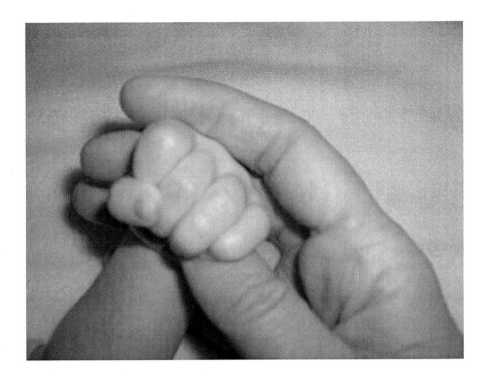

Preschool

'Mamma, when I'm at school and you're at work,
my hands will miss your hair;
when you're at work and I'm at school,
I will miss you all day'
Your tender limbs press against me,
small hands stroking my hair.

'Mamma, when I'm at school and you're at work,
I will miss your eyes;
when you're at work and I'm at school,
I will miss you all day'
Your friends take you to the window;
You wave, watching with large eyes as I drive away.

Dressing

Small slumbering body stirs, groans as the blinds open
Big smile as arms reach to be held
Warm cheek presses against mine, 'Morning Mamma'

Groggy, unsteady feet reach down for pant legs
Still-clumsy hands reach up for sweater arms
Unruly curls press against my face, 'Thank you Mamma'

Hug

Cool Fall morning, shoes are on, jacket is on
teeth are brushed, vita-gummy is chewed
The gang is ready to get in the car

Small boy smiles: 'Hug for Mamma'; Dad grins: 'Pappa too!'
'Now all together!'. Small boy squeezes inbetween Mom and Dad
Warm joy surrounds us in our family hug

Mamma's Work

You smile at me with Scallywag eyes
Mamma, when I grow up, can I work too?"
I grin, "Of course you can, work is fun."
Your eyes sparkle:
'Mamma, I want to do what you do'
I beam, you reach out and your arms circle my neck:
'Mamma, can I work with you?'
'Yes, my love, come, let's type together'

Bath

Pearly droplets sparkle in unruly curls
Fluffy foam clings to smooth pink knees
Plump, animated hands splash,
scatter the frothy bubbles on the floor

Wash cloth flies up and sits smacked against the wall
Sponge animals cavort down in the water
Mom's shirt is soaked, small voice fills the room,
Dad peeks, grinning, at the door

Multi-mom

Gymnastics

You join the class alone and smile at new friends
Three-year-old eagerness in bright eyes
Take your turn to jump and tumble
No fear or thought of Mom and Dad
who proudly watch as your independence grows
Mom takes a picture as you swing on rings
beaming as your small hands hold on
After the class you run to my arms
'Mom, that was fun!'

Dinosaurs

Shiny, brown, stone bones reach high
Pieced together in a paleo-puzzle
Tell a story of a lost world

Young boy gazes up, eyes wide
'Pappa, is that a diplodocus?'
'Mamma, can I see one with skin on?'

Music Lesson

Circle of friends, giggling, clapping,
wide-eyed at colourful toys
Young faces laughing, singing
eager for a turn on the xylophone

Hands and feet tap the beat
Melody starts, changes
Small arms wide, birds fly
Small legs pump, kangaroos jump

Sing and fly, laugh and jump, young ones,
feel the joy of the music.

Monarchs

Plump caterpillars striped in yellow and black, crawl up
Gnaw at the veins of spurge leaves to let the milky sap flow down
Greedy larvae gorge and swell, pupate into silent still nymphs

Kindergarten biologists watch with eager eyes,
"Are they growing?" ; gently keep them covered
As they hang on branches in their safe dome

On a September morning, tubal chrysalides split open
black and orange wings emerge, crumpled at first,
fill and fan, revealing its splendour for a few moments,
then flutter free

Snowsuit

Blue and yellow, green and grey
Plaid pattern spells snow fun
Padded inside, waterproof,
Little-boy-proof

Cozy hoodie keeps small head toasty
Elastic bottoms keep small legs dry
Zip him up, mitttens on -
"Pappa, I need the bathroom!"

Bedtime Books

Lured by your sponge toys, you happily hop in the bath
Enticed by a promise of stories, you clamber out with me
I snuggle you in a fluffy towel, cream up the squirming body,
Time for a few books before bed

Finally dressed, you sway with me in our rocking chair,
Eyes wide, you read with me about Angel Fish, Orcas and Belugas
Yawning, you listen to stories about Elephants, Zebras and Giraffe,
We click off the light, and still swaying, small hand holds my hair,
small eyes slowly close

Multi-Mom

You busily play, dismantling your latest train set
I sit nearby, planning our meals for the coming week
I use my BlackBerry to store my shopping list, like an alpha-geek

School menus for busy bodies are available to download
Mom can plan ahead, multi-task less, enjoy you more
Finally with list and menu saved, I can head to the store

You enjoy your noisy play, a strategy game with your dad
BlackBerry recipes in hand, I can quietly cook for the week
I`m just an ordinary multi-mom, you`re the true young geek

Do Life with Me

Morning Coffee

Stumble down the stairs
Fumble for the light
Slowly emerge from another night
Nuke a cup of water
See the world at six
Scribble a few lines and sip the foamy fix

Angel

I think you hide wings under your shirt
Although I`ve never seen you fly
My helper, partner, friend
Comforter when I cry

From diapers to mopping and laundry
You`ve done it all
Tender, committed Dad
You`re always on call

I know you hide wings under your shirt
You never let us cry
My helper, partner, friend
My angel, you let me fly high

Parenting

You test us, challenge us, make us smile;
You try us, delight us when you enjoy your meal;
You teach us more about truth and trust
and give us an excuse to munch finger foods.

Flux

The early morning wakes me, let's get ready for the week
I work downstairs as you and Pappa sleep
prepare a quick breakfast, thinking about what to wear

quietly I shower, get ready for the day
Pappa stirs a little as I dry my hair
finally ready, I softly kiss him awake

he groans: "Where are you going so early on a Sunday?"
I look in the mirror, exhale
it's not Monday, it's sweet, slow, Sunday…

School starts

Breakfast with Dad while Mom prepares lunch,
Dear Dad is patient while you slowly munch,
Off to school to meet new friends,
You run and start playing with the boisterous bunch

Flatbread and Curry

Silky chewy milky dough
mix and knead and roll

braise till bubbly brown and crisp
one by one they go

Soft and buttery, tear and dip
scoop curry from the bowl

family gather, pass the plates
whiffs of goodness, ohhhh

Feast Table

In our new home we will have a long table
Twelve chairs to gather loved ones from near and far
Serious serial cooking by everyone
Serious serial feasting and tall tales
Come take your seat at the table in our new home.

Game

Riding on two-headed turtles,
you explore forests of flimsy ferns
Running in a meadow of wildflowers
You fight an enemy with mystical powers

"Mamma, if we help the bad guys, they will love us,
If we are good to them, they will be good like us"
My boy, believe in the power of your magic
Be who you are, a force for good

Forest Walk

Asters, Roberts and Garlic Mustards,
Oxeye Daisies and Ladies' Tresses;
We stroll under tall trees
Touching and sniffing eagerly

Goldenrod, Silverrod, Witch Hazel;
Late afternoon sun speckles through the trees
You ride on Pappa's shoulders,
squealing as spider webs touch your face

Chickweed, Coneflower, wild carrot;
Family with stroller and large poodle pass by,
Young people see us at the river, smile:
"Boy, you've got it good!"

Fall

Quiet forest sighs, reaches up, pulls back its strength to the roots
Leaves slowly wither,
flutter down to make a speckled carpet of colour
You run, scatter the leaves with eager feet,
stoop down to pick up a bright red one, larger than your face.
We carry it home, press it between pages in a heavy book,
a keepsake of this time, this Fall.

Pumpkin Farm

Ride and sing-a-long with teachers and friends
Voices rise as the bus goes round the bends
Tags on wrists to keep young charges safe,
Active bodies bundle out to explore

Young calf, piglets and a donkey too,
Harvest pumpkins and a hay-ride, woohoo!
After a cool Fall day filled with fun
Boy is asleep sooner than ever before

Partner

My partner, friend, gentleman
You are my gentle man
In good times and hard times
you give us all you can

Together we raise our David
Guide him on his way
Together we make a life
filled with fun and play

My partner, friend and gentleman
You are my gentle man
You bring so much more to the world
More than I ever can

Becoming

Growing

You're only four years old
Already my heart is in my mouth
Hopeful but sometimes terrified
that one misstep will let all go South

You start to assert your own view
So young and yet strong-willed
I just keep smiling through it all
Trusting your dreams will be fulfilled

You're only four years old
I know you won't go wrong
Humour hides my fear and dread
And Hope will keep me strong

New Day

Early morning, your giggles fill the room
as characters cavort across the screen
Mamma works in the kitchen,
lets Pappa snore and dream

Small body sits quietly on the couch,
snug in red pajama suit
Big eyes smile at me
as I prepare porridge and fruit

Early morning, your belly-laugh fills the room
As Tom and Jerry play and fight
You finish your breakfast happily
I'm thankful, the day will be alright

A Boy's Prayer

As our car comes to a halt at your school
You ask that we wait before the day starts
You want to pray for your teachers, before you go

Outside is the cool early morning, windows slightly fogged
Warm inside the car, we sit snug in our coats
You pray to 'Father God' and say thanks for 'such a nice school'

Your clear voice fills the car, as you pray for the work day too
Pappa and Mamma have a lump in the throat
Our eyes meet for a moment, before you go

Spoon Snuggle

The park next door is silent in the autumn air
you call to me in the early hours
we snuggle in the quiet darkness, safe and warm

You bury your four-year-old hand in my hair
my hand reaches, feels still-baby-soft skin
Soothing comfort of a fluffy duvet surrounds us

The forest outside stirs in the autumn wind
you call to me with your small knowing voice
Folded together, we drift to sleep in the darkness, safe and warm

Puzzles

Fall air stirs the bare branches outside
My boys are engrossed in their play
Dad builds a huge landscape scene,
son his favourite 'Cars' here inside

Sweet, mellow Sunday night togetherness
Family time after a busy week
I watch them, tasting their delicious nearness

Night comes, cloaks the bare branches outside
Here my boys are content as they play
Son builds three pictures on his own, eyes bright with pride

Maze

From yellow to orange to purple and green
This orb is a spatial learning machine

Small ball runs on tracks in the maze
Don't let it drop! What a fun new craze

Small hands hold and turn the sphere
Small eyes fixed, "Mamma,please help me here!"

From yellow to orange to purple and green
For six to sixty, a brain bending machine

Insects

You quietly watch your Planet Earth
Riveted by the lives and doings of bugs
From damselflies with gossamer wings
To Dawson's bees and slugs

Japanese Red Bug mother
Works non-stop day after day
You ask why the mommy bug dies
I hug you, not sure what to say

You quietly watch your Planet Earth
Riveted, although you've seen it before
'Mamma, will we also die?'
'We'll sing with the angels forevermore'

Light

You crawl into your small black tent
draw pictures with fluorescent pen-light
crescents, stars and space ships
dance in the dark of the night

I crawl in the tent with you
hold the forms for you just right
We laugh at the strange shapes
For a moment we hug tight

Lets crawl into your small black tent
draw pictures with fluorescent pen-light
moons, cars and dinosaurs
dance in the dark of the night

Halloween

Chocolate balls, jawbreakers, ghostly gum
for witches, goblins and monsters, Boo!
a night of lights and colourful treats
for princesses, frogs and Spiderman too

You wear your green monster horns to school
Eager to share with your friend
Squealing characters run around
Dressing up for the day is the trend

I hope the night will be filled with fun
for princesses, frogs and Spiderman too
soon you will be too grown up for the treats
for witches, goblins and monsters, Boo!

Misty Morning

The forest near the river seems to whisper
Nearly nude trees barely visible in the cool fog
My boots crunch on dry leaves
From the haze appear a boy and a dog

Soft pink cheeks flushed with the night's warmth
you slumber snugly in your 'Car' bed
Pappa is in the shower
under the cover stirs a curly sleepy head

The forest near the river seems to whisper
A boy whistles to a boisterous dog
The doorknob squeaks as I step inside
Safe here from cool frost and fog

Cousin

Dear cousin with flame-red hair
you've known me since I was born
your messages of quiet strength
embraced me in every storm

On birthdays and holidays and everyday days
you send me news and more
on high days and low days
I reclaim your words from before

Someone who is a world away
can be closer than those who are near
you are just a word away
you are here in spirit, my dear.

Work-out

morning routine of the muscular kind
pull out the mat while the boys still snore
stretch the tendons before the daily grind
my favourite muscle is my mind

Wild World

Programmer

Sound and colour dance while I struggle to make sense
Objects and connections, data volumes are immense
Craft and wrought the logic, test the concepts through
Mind, heart and hands unite, to build something new

Farmer

Early morning hours, read and research
companies and trusts to find the best
use the dividend to re-invest
my modest crop grows, time will do the rest

Seven

Nascent, reconstructed
from strangers to friends,
newcomers, then residents,
built from tenants to owners,
moved from immigrants to citizens,
grew from partners to parents,
visitors to voters, in seven years

View

Behind our office building, the silent forest is in full colour
As Fall peaks, the tall trees are slowly becoming bare
Many colleagues visit our team to discuss projects
All comment on the glorious view that we share

Rainy Friday morning, Blackberry problems are restored
Four days of concern, finally good news after bad
Still our company is led by a great team
filled with confidence and strength, what a week they've had

Behind our office building, the silent forest is in full colour
As Winter approaches, the tall trees become bare
Many colleagues visit us
Simply to see the glorious, fleeting view that we share

Markets

Money, money makes the world go round
`Shall we invest in Dollar or in Pound?
Inflation, recession the wolf`s at the door
We stick to our budget to save more

Risk and reward, drives the greed
Little thought for those in need,
Financiers get paid a stack
Who will care for those who lack?

Money, money makes the world go round
Shall we invest in Dollar or in Pound?
Inflation, recession, we can save more
We can donate, keep the wolf from the world`s door.

Flex

What shall we do with the configuration, optimization,
Flexibility fixation
Super duper systems
An exercise in frustration

Maintain and sustain
Keep it running, so mundane
Don`t over-design
keep changes benign

What shall we do with the configuration, optimization
Flexibility fixation,
Super duper systems
A study in complexification

War ends

Nine years of struggle
Conflict not of our making
Soldiers tried to bring order
While Qaeda lurks at Pakistan border

The age of America comes to an end
Weakened by overspending and debt
Canada adapts to a new world order
Supporting our friends south of the border

Nine years of struggle and waste
Brings America to its knees
Brave soldiers tried to bring order
But danger still lurks at every border

Bail-Outs

World economy on the brink
Strong countries brought to their knees
Population aging in the West
A new world order, but nobody sees

Developing world comes to mind
Nascent countries were helped before
Now the older nations ask
Time to knock on a younger door

World economy may still sink
High winds will fell the higher trees
A lost decade may still loom
The New World can save, if only it sees

Roam with Me

Allegany

From Buffalo and Orchard Park
all the way down the 219
the road is mine, New York State is mine

Through Ellicottville and Little valley,
the road through Salamanca
brings us to Allegany

Towering giants display their Fall splendour
We hike for miles and enjoy a picnic on the trail

From Buffalo and Orchard Park
all the way down the 219
New York State and Pennsylvania are mine

Morning Hike

Early morning sunlight speckles through the trees,
Yellow orange and red Fall-coloured leaves.

We take the winding trail up the mountainside,
You give your Dad a workout: piggy-back ride.

We scramble over rocks, follow a stream
This magical togetherness the answer to a dream.

Ellicottville

From Jefferson Street to Elizabeth,
from Dina's in downtown to Tops Up,
you opened your arms to the smiling, feasting crowds.

From fried dough to rainbow snowcones and fudge
we worked our way through arts and crafts stalls
offering everything from the quaint to the divine

E'ville, your sunshine warmed us,
lulling babies in strollers and grannies with walkers;

Your music enthralled us, colourful houses called us,
Whether winter fun or Fall Festival,
we'll be back next year.

Thanksgiving

From Good Waterloo to Fort Erie, we take the road south,
across the Rainbow Bridge, we enter the State of Bad Coffee
You enjoy your donut with sprinkles,
while Mom and Dad let the brew go...

Our last warm days are spent around the Allegany,
taking in Fall and small-town charms
Our first trip abroad as Canadians leaves us content
but thankful to be home
You sing along with your 'car songs',
tired after a long weekend of hiking, festivals and colours.

Halifax Memories

At Martinique Beach we had a stroll
And took a drive through towns we love
At Crystal Crescent we played in the sand
And stood on the rocks at Peggy's Cove

Dinner for five at the Wooden Monkey
Long walk along the pier
Streets filled with buskers and smiles
Blue bay sparkling, blue sky clear

At Martinique Beach we will have a swim
And come back to the towns we love
At Crystal Crescent we will picnic in the sand
Next year we'll play again at Peggy's Cove

Tagore: Peaceful Home

Baby's Way

If baby only wanted to, he could fly up to heaven this moment.
It is not for nothing that he does not leave us.
He loves to rest his head on mother's bosom,
and cannot ever bear to lose sight of her.
Baby knows all manner of wise words,
though few on earth can understand their meaning.

It is not for nothing that he never wants to speak.
The one thing he wants is to learn mother's words
from mother's lips.
That is why he looks so innocent.

Baby had a heap of gold and pearls,
yet he came like a beggar on to this earth.
It is not for nothing he came in such a disguise.
This dear little naked mendicant pretends to be utterly helpless,
so that he may beg for mother's wealth of love.

Baby was so free from every tie
in the land of the tiny crescent moon.
It was not for nothing he gave up his freedom.
He knows that there is room for endless joy
in mother's little corner of a heart,
and it is sweeter far than liberty to be caught
and pressed in her dear arms.

Baby never knew how to cry. He dwelt in the land of perfect bliss.
It is not for nothing he has chosen to shed tears.
Though with the smile of his dear face he draws
mother's yearning heart to him, yet his little cries
over tiny troubles weave the double bond of pity and love.

The Home

I paced alone on the road across the field while the sunset was hiding its last gold like a miser.

The daylight sank deeper and deeper into the darkness, and the widowed land, whose harvest had been reaped, lay silent.

Suddenly a boy's shrill voice rose into the sky. He traversed the dark unseen, leaving the track of his song across the hush of the evening.

His village home lay there at the end of the waste land, beyond the sugar-cane field, hidden among the shadows of the banana and the slender areca palm, the cocoa-nut and the dark green jack-fruit trees.

I stopped for a moment in my lonely way under the starlight, and saw spread before me the darkened earth surrounding with her arms countless homes furnished with cradles and beds, mothers' hearts and evening lamps, and young lives glad with a gladness that knows nothing of its value for the world.

When and Why

When I bring you coloured toys, my child, I understand why there is such a play of colours on clouds, on water, and why flowers are painted in tints—when I give coloured toys to you, my child.

When I sing to make you dance, I truly know why there is music in leaves, and why waves send their chorus of voices to the heart of the listening earth—when I sing to make you dance.

When I bring sweet things to your greedy hands, I know why there is honey in the cup of the flower, and why fruits are secretly filled with sweet juice—when I bring sweet things to your greedy hands.

When I kiss your face to make you smile, my darling, I surely understand what pleasure streams from the sky in morning light, and what delight the summer breeze brings to my body—when I kiss you to make you smile.

Tagore: Flowers of Joy

The First Jasmines

Ah, these jasmines, these white jasmines!

I seem to remember the first day
when I filled my hands with these jasmines, these white jasmines.
I have loved the sunlight, the sky and the green earth;
I have heard the liquid murmur of the river
through the darkness of midnight;

Autumn sunsets have come to me at the bend of a road
in the lonely waste, like a bride raising her veil to accept her lover.
Yet my memory is still sweet
with the first white jasmines that I held in my hand
when I was a child.

Many a glad day has come in my life,
and I have laughed with merrymakers on festival nights.
On grey mornings of rain I have crooned many an idle song.
I have worn round my neck the evening wreath of bakulas
woven by the hand of love.
Yet my heart is sweet with the memory of the first fresh jasmines
that filled my hands when I was a child.

The Gift

I want to give you something, my child,
for we are drifting in the stream of the world.
Our lives will be carried apart, and our love forgotten.
But I am not so foolish as to hope that I could buy your heart
with my gifts.

Young is your life, your path long,
and you drink the love we bring you at one draught
and turn and run away from us.
You have your play and your playmates.
What harm is there if you have no time or thought for us.

We, indeed, have leisure enough in old age
to count the days that are past, to cherish in our hearts
what our hands have lost for ever.
The river runs swift with a song,
breaking through all barriers.
But the mountain stays and remembers,
and follows her with his love.

Tagore: Grace and Freedom

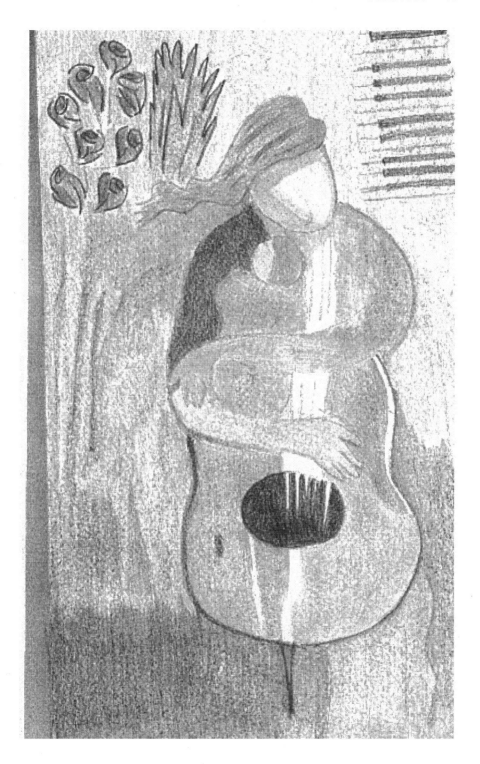

My Song

This song of mine will wind its music around you, my child,
like the fond arms of love.
This song of mine will touch your forehead like a kiss of blessing.

When you are alone it will sit by your side and whisper in your ear,
when you are in the crowd it will fence you about with aloofness.

My song will be like a pair of wings to your dreams,
it will transport your heart to the verge of the unknown.

It will be like the faithful star overhead
when dark night is over your road.
My song will sit in the pupils of your eyes,
and will carry your sight into the heart of things.
And when my voice is silent in death,
my song will speak in your living heart.

The Last Bargain

"Come and hire me," I cried, while in the morning I was walking
on the stone-paved road.
Sword in hand, the King came in his chariot.
He held my hand and said, "I will hire you with my power."
But his power counted for nought, and he went away in his chariot.

In the heat of the midday the houses stood with shut doors.
I wandered along the crooked lane.
An old man came out with his bag of gold.
He pondered and said, "I will hire you with my money."
He weighed his coins one by one, but I turned away.

It was evening. The garden hedge was all aflower.
The fair maid came out and said, "I will hire you with a smile."
Her smile paled and melted into tears,
and she went back alone into the dark.

The sun glistened on the sand, and the sea waves broke waywardly.
A child sat playing with shells.
He raised his head and seemed to know me,
and said, "I hire you with nothing."
From thenceforward that bargain struck in child's play
made me a free man.